WE ARE ALL POEMS

WE ARE ALL POEMS

KATHERINE NORTH

for my Wildest one, who is a poem indeed

I'm hosting a banquet.
Everyone's invited.
Come sit at my table with me.
Oh look...
here they come.

THE ONE WITH A LETTER FROM MANAGEMENT

Dear reader, it says,
She would like you to know
that this is not an accurate or even fair
—wait—
beautiful,
beloved people
—blah blah—
no I'm not reading this,
so much apology energy,
I'm going to crumple it up
because the whole point
is to say the things.
Let them just say the Things.

THE CRUMPLED UP LETTER

~~Dear reader,~~
~~I would like you to know~~
~~that this is not an accurate or even fair~~
~~depiction of my life. A life which is beautiful,~~
~~a life I love, full of beloved people~~
~~and a garden and a house by the sea.~~
~~These are the transcription of an interior conversation~~
~~that never saw the light of day~~
~~during the hardest time, a time when true love~~
~~transformed me from a solo city mom~~
~~to a suburban married mother of five almost overnight.~~
~~And furthermore it was also when I realized~~
~~that there was no book deal, no agent,~~
~~no publisher who was going to save me~~
~~or even alter the trajectory of my life~~
~~as I had once thought. All my plans broke.~~
~~I fell off the edge of my own life.~~
~~Still I trudged forward in desperation,~~
~~because I love these people so much,~~
~~no even more than that— so very *very* much~~
~~it's so important you understand that—~~
~~but in the process some parts of me~~
~~went into hiding.~~

And that's who is invited
to this banquet in particular—
the ones who went away, to finally say
the Things
they couldn't say before.

THE ONE WHO GAVE BIRTH TWICE

It took longer to birth myself
than it took to birth my daughter—
the caul
between me and myself
thickest of all.

THE ONE WHO WILL BE AN APPLE TREE

When I am gone, plant an apple tree
over my body or at least
over my memory.
Let me keep turning through the seasons:
let me give it all up in winter,
dance a pink froth in spring,
let me swell round and crimson
to feed my beloveds and gnarl down
my roots to feed my next green.
Let me grow ripe and heavy again and again
so when the last fruit is gone
and I lose everything
you'll still find me
in bushel baskets and cold cellars,
in ciders and pies and seeds.
Let me live on as
a dusty jar of applesauce
on your pantry shelf—
a lingering sweetness.

THE ONE WHO WANTS EVERYTHING

I'm only asking for
one piece in
The New Yorker, just one
little New York Times bestseller,
just one tiny giant social media following.
I only need one real
Diane Von Furstenburg dress,
one simple sprawling Victorian farmhouse
with heritage gardens and built-in bookcases,
just one hit of fame and prestige,
just one bank account sturdy enough
to weather
life
just one moment
when we know
for sure
that we are all okay.
That we are not embarrassing.

THE LONELY ONE

In my new city where I have no friends
I lie in a hot bath listening
to the bus so close to my head
holding a cold green bottle of Portland
reading about green gables
and silver birches.
My little girl is finally asleep,
and I am alone
as I have been all day, all week, all month, all year.
In this new place I'm spinning
a wild idea into groceries and clean sheets,
knitting sheer daring into
a golden apartment and a couch with pink flowers on it.
My comfort is this nightly bath.
It is the only place I talk to anyone
even if it is just my own
9 year old self
who read the same book twenty-five years ago
and also longed for puffed sleeves
and didn't yet have daring,
or beer, or permission.
In the bath she whispers back,
Anyway, I'm still here.
You still have me.

THE ONE IN THE YELLOW DRESS

I shall pour
dandelion tea into
pink china teacups
and on my windowsill floats
a red geranium in a cracked pot
and my butter
lives in a butter dish
that is robin's egg blue.
I make friends with local pansies
and swoon at all peonies
and buzz at the thought of
flowers growing from my own garden one day
but I'm not waiting.
Why would I wait?
I went ahead and communed with dusty peach joy
blooming in my imagination,
already dreamed up roses
from the muddiest dirt,
and together we are
greening out,
humming gold honey hums,
greeting beauty
like our oldest friend.

THE ONE WHO WRITES THINGS DOWN

'Tis I! It's me.
The one with the big muscles
holding back
the great grasses of the prairie,
singlehandedly holding apart the wild waves
of the sea
holding on for dear life
as life crashes over,
as the words threaten to scatter;
I am the one who parts the needy crowds
— *SORRY*, I say—
but I am not sorry
EXCUSE ME
COMING THROUGH
and you'll follow gratefully behind
because
THIS IS AN EMERGENCY
and I am the one
indeed
who is SAVING LIVES AROUND HERE.

THE ONE WHO BROKE HER OWN WATERS

When I was fearless
I wore a coat made of peacock blue silk
and tromped around the city in delicate wing-heels
but also sat up terrified
so many nights in my tiny studio
curled in shame
soaked in resistance
dreading the membrane
between me and my work—
how it had to breached,
a hot gush
before I could breathe.

THE ONE CALLED RESILIENCE

Is it ever going to be me?
The world shakes its head.
No, not you. Never you.
But I ignore them.
Ask myself, answer,
make my own damn echo.
It's going to be me.
One day.
It's going to be me.

THE ONE WITH THE AXE

Don't be afraid
of me, though I am indeed
the wild-eyed one with an axe,
the one you've heard about,
and yes my jeans are muddy
and my hair has gone swampy
but mostly I am just
frantic with dismay
at how things have gone
sideways.
How far you let it go.
So I am here to help
in the only way possible.
Let's chop it all down.
Forest, house, bridge, fence,
bangs, gas lines.
Let's cut you free.
I'm coming, baby.

THE ONE WHO HAS BEEN TO THERAPY

Thank you, dearheart,
truly,
but we don't need that axe—
at least not today, honestly,
if you could just set it down—
but I appreciate
your clear plan— here, I'll
just take it from you—
but I promise I'll keep it safe
and if we ever do need to
chop it all down
then darling
you'll be the
very first one I'll call.

THE ONE WHO IS ALWAYS SO SAD

Let me in.
You didn't send me
an invitation.
I'm here anyway.
Wait, I'm not here to ruin things.
Reach for my hands, here,
feel the jolt:
a hum
that animates everything.
The old metal fan shyly grinning, now
the begonia waving her arms wildly in recognition—
I'm telling you
what you call sadness
is also our portal
to saturated presence.
Call it
the place of the humming or
just fully human-ing.
Sometimes, listen,
shhh— I am the only way
you can get to bliss.
Don't be afraid of my blue dress.
I'll pull it aside to show you
the sky inside everything.

THE ONE WHO CAN HEAL THINGS

WITH HER HANDS

(She hasn't actually come out yet,
but we know she's there—
we can hear her
humming
her little hum.)

THE ONE WHO MELTS

Everywhere, brimming over
at the worst times, trembling lip —stop it—
eyes spilling, I know,
I'm the embarrassing great aunt
who insists on coming with you
to the mall in my beige socks and
buckled shoes.
Honey, you look just beautiful
in that dress.
What you don't know
is that when I melt,
I can go anywhere.
Salt and water
trickling along invisible
arteries,
ley lines of feeling,
zinging cords to the sky,
all those embarrassing
puddles
are magical conduits
hooking me up
to
oh, everything.

THE ONE WHO FELL IN LOVE

Oh this is why they call it falling,
I thought, as I went down.
I didn't even think it was a real thing,
falling,
I thought everyone was faking,
Look, mom, watch me flail!
I'd never looked in someone's eyes
and thought— *oh hello,*
there you are.
Then I am angry:
I have been waiting so long for you!
All those years I thought you didn't exist.
Now here you are.
And miraculously, you recognize me too.
Everything shifts,
and I am falling, falling, falling
—do you think this is
our tenth lifetime? millionth?—
anyway, it's clear that we are
always and forever
and even after that.

THE ONE WHO LIVES IN
SCARCITY, ALBERTA

There is never enough
time
money
energy
sex
solitude
toilet paper
never ever
enough.
This is my town.
I have lived here for years.
I've been here so long that
unfortunately now
it lives in me.

THE ONE WHO'S HEARD OF
ANOTHER PLACE

I haven't just heard of it,
I've glimpsed it,
heard its murmur,
felt it rise up on my tongue
like a honey homeland.
A state of enoughness:
a basket of apples,
a herd of children,
a village of trees.
Walking to a quiet house,
steam rising from the tea.
Look—
enoughness lives here too,
and I will curl up
round as the moon
and sleep in her generous branches.

THE ONE WHO NEEDS ALONE TIME

Someone stops my new husband on the street
to commiserate
about his horrible wife,
going off on a selfish awful rude solo retreat
without him— who does that?
Me, I do,
because I love us with my whole heart
and see I'm pouring out every drop
and I'd do it a thousand times over
but I love me too
I do
so I have to run away
to the cool lakes
and the pools and the
fountains and the rivers where it rains
so I don't dry up and blow away
so I don't turn to prairie dust
so I can do what I yearn to do
which is to still be me
and have a full heart to love with,
which is to say
to stay.

THE ONE WHO IS SUCH A BITCH

Really you should love me the most,
the armor that holds
all our jelly together,
the stiff edges
you can pour yourself into
so you don't drip all
everywhere—
my spikes
a halo,
beloved patron saint
of underdogs
with my scary sword
always
saving sticky spots
from the kitchen floor
uttering the forbidden word
(boundaries)
and sending them back
to try again.

THE CAPABLE ONE WHO
GETS IT ALL DONE

Pushing the wagon up the hill
is hard work, especially when
they keep adding rocks to it.
Still, look at my muscle.
It's an honor, apparently.
So I grit my teeth,
dig deeper,
stay up later,
push harder,
sit down and cry sometimes.
Stand up and yell sometimes.
They tell me to smile more,
enjoy the moment,
don't be so sharp.
Think about your husband,
he has needs, you know.
So I sigh and take a step toward the showers.
—Right, also the wagon.
Of course the wagon.
Always the wagon.

There is someone here
in a strange dress
who says
she would like to take me
to a room full of books
with no wagons and no rocks.
She offers to rub my feet
and pour me tea
and put a velvet cushion
under my head and
read me poetry.
But then—
if I let down my guard for a minute—
who would push the wagon?
The one with my beloved
children in it?

THE ONE WHO IS OFF TWIRLING

Kindred spirit
in the twilight
unashamed of her earnesty
or anything really, a wonder—
she wanders away from
our raucous table but
she will drift back
with her arms full of apple blossoms
so leave her in the twilight, let her be
oh she
of the starry eyes
and gritty hope—
the one we recognized, remember?
in all the books?
never seeing
dusty pages were a mirror
for our own forgotten stars.

THE FARMWIFE

Into the stockpot,
that'll be soup.
Give me your wilted celery,
your old onions,
those shriveled carrots.
Show me your cracked suitcase
of faded hopes and
worn-out flimsy dreams
and I'll turn them into a quilt
for cold nights.
I'll watch over you
as you dream,
as the compost turns itself
into everything possible.
They rolled their eyes
at my apron, but I hold
seeds in one pocket,
and in the other,
an egg still warm.

THE ONE WHO WAKES WITH DREAD

I woke this morning
like most
full of dread and sorrow
dragged my sorry ass out of bed
walked to the mirror and said
Why aren't you happy
look at this
life
please appreciate it
and my heart cried
but I don't know how
and my head wailed
how will we pay the bills
and my soul whispered
shhhhh, be here.
When I pray I pray
to the universe
but also
I am afraid that the universe
will be angry at me for
not being more grateful, for not
appreciating this bountiful
beautiful life, this love,
these children, and so

in order to give me
a purer kind of joy which is to say pain
it will smite me— kill my children,
take my life from me, drop a tree
on the roof—
and then only in retrospect will I appreciate it
only then will I say
I guess I was happy and didn't even know it.
Madre says,
That is a terrible and stupid story.
Tell a better one.

THE ONE WHO IS BAD

I like everything bad,
pink carpets that are impractical
and silk dresses that are outlandish
and diamonds
and the feeling between my legs
at night.
My hair was the wrong color and
my skin was too pale and now I have
too many opinions and somehow
I'm still a foreigner.
Eternal *gaijin*.
I am a home wrecker,
also.
Even though I just breathed
and a house of sticks fell down
and inside the wreckage was— my beloved.
Still
I am selfish,
I like solitude,
I hate playing board games and
I want to have sex only once a month;
I want my mouth to be my own,

I want to buy champagne
and books and let the children
go hungry.
I want to drop my wagon
and walk to a cave above the ocean
and be wicked, so wicked
with my writing and my meditating and my silence
all my evil days.

THE ONE WHO TRIES TO BE
GOOD ENOUGH TO COMPENSATE

I will be so good, I will
be the best mother, best wife, best lover,
best do-gooder. You will see
that I am beyond reproach.
I will do everything perfectly
even if I am gasping
so that I can point at what my
bad self created— this family, this home,
this love, this art— and say,
Isn't it good? Isn't it good enough?

THE ONE WHO POURS THE WINE

Oh yes, blame me,
wicked woman grabbing
bottle and glass—
here, I'll pour you solace and shame—
but look,
I am filling up the red wine
in your veins,
I'm only replacing what you keep
glugging into
everyone else.
Without me
you'd fall over,
heart chambers pale and empty.
Stop leeching your
lifeblood out then,
so I can fucking stop pouring.
Believe me—
I would love to stop pouring.

THE ONE PERCHED ON MY CHEST

WITH CLAWS

Before you can even talk to me
you have to ask me
to loosen my grip
on your chest
because I cannot stop
clutching at
your lung tendrils
and squeezing.
Let go, you can say,
and I might nod but I am lying.
But if you can hold your arms
in a crook and show me,
I will clamber out and curl up
there in the circle of you
like a tiny spiky moon.
If you let me cocoon there, if you wrap me
in tenderness and a thin shawl
I will rock myself
back and forth
while showing you metaphors
about butterflies and life cycles
and when I stick my head out
damp and sweaty

to whisper,
Let me go,
you have to understand
that for me to transform
into my next self—
for me to imago into a phoenix—
you have to let me blow away.
Take a deep breath.
Do the maternal sway.
Now I sit in a meadow
gazing out
next to someone
and we both
think quiet thoughts
about crossing over,
and who we are now,
and who we left behind.

THE ONE WHO IS A FALCON

Snap.
Here I am, slightest noise,
on alert, hyper vigilant.
Crackle.
Here comes someone,
they will need something,
so I take the soft presence of us
and I fold it down
like the top of a chip bag,
rolling it down til
I can perch on it.
Pop.
The door is opening.
How do they feel?
Are they sad? Angry? Dangerous? Happy?
Which version of me should I leave
on display
before I fly away?

THE ONE WHO REMEMBERS
IMPOSSIBLE THINGS

I remember things
I am not supposed to,
lives that weren't ours,
memories we didn't live.
Other things, too.
I could show you.
I could show you everything.

ON BEHALF OF THE ONE WHO
DIDN'T GET
THE EXACT RIGHT PRESENT

Stop scolding her.
She already knows she is ridiculous—
precious privileged princess brat.
Look what she is holding out
for you to see:
old hurts, bits of barbed wire,
fishhooks she pulled out of us
and kept cupped in her hands
all this time
taking their hurt for us.
This is her invitation to melt them down.
Tears work best.
If you let her, she will turn this handful
of dangerous wire
into something
else entirely, something maybe even
precious.

THE ALIEN SCIENTIST OBSERVER

I notice that the human
releases HAPPY waves
when focusing on the rain,
but PANIC waves
when the thought-form of taxes
touch the circuits
even in a brief thought.
And yet the subject is lying
in the same bed
in the same physical position
when both of these things happen.
What conclusions can we draw from this?
—but the rest of us break in:—
SHUT UP.
We're trying to listen to the rain.

THE ONE WHO'S STILL 18,

WITH THE STACK OF MANILA ENVELOPES

Great, I'm the hero
who sprung you,
mailed off packets to the fancy universities,
(don't forget it was mostly Mom)
holding the weight of the paper that
bought your ticket
to another world.
It was too much,
too scary, too sharp,
but there was nothing else to be done
so I learned to bite down harder,
press until I broke,
stay up all night, bear down,
grind through, keep pushing
until something cracked.
I found a thousand ways to break.
The snap of broken bone.
Crunched knuckle.
Cracked tooth.
It's okay. It was the only way.
This is how we made it through.
The world was so hard,
and we were so spindly.

But listen to me now, dammit—
now you are
TOO OLD
to still be
breaking shit.
Okay?

THE COUNCIL STOPS TO CONFER

Therefore let it be decreed:
Let us watch over her,
for she is still mostly a child.
Let us learn to do without destroying.
Let us be the grownup
who tells the little ones to
go rest, go soak, go float,
because we've got this.
She can stand down.
We have come to a decision.
We hereby declare that we shall
learn to be an adult
without
breaking anything,
especially me.

THE ONE WHO PLAYED SECRETARY

Mortified
doesn't even begin
to describe my
suede pumps, navy suit,
stockings.
Down the hall
is a woman
who attended the same university
I did— has the same four-year education—
but she is the most junior hire
on the real track, the
career track.
And I am a secretary.
I order the coffee.
She looks at me with curiosity and pity:
what happened?
I do not know what happened.
What secret memo I missed.
So when I see her in the halls,
I duck.
I don't know if it's worse
that I am losing this game
or that no one else even knows
I was trying to play.

THE ONE IN THE CHEAP GOLD SHOES

I take all the dutiful
walks by the river
with his family
like a good sport
and they worry about my feet
in my cheap high-heeled
gold sandals
but I can walk for miles
on that plastic with its maternal sway;
I can blur their good intentions
into a sound like the wind,
I can feel something billow
and swell
because down below
a steady gold
glints and flashes,
with each step
urging me
to walk on,
farther
then away.

THE ONE WHO IS CAUTIOUS

WITH HER OWN SPARKLE

Once I was singing a little song
to myself
dancing a little dance
and the words came like a slap:
You think you're pretty special, don't you?
I didn't, I was just twirling,
but now that you mention it, why I am
rather sparkly.
I wish I'd moved to LA for
my big shot, I wish I'd tried out
for Broadway, I wish I'd kept dancing
or learned to play guitar but mostly
that my writing sparkled enough
that the whole world would see it.
Sometimes a dark shawl
comes over me.
Sometimes that was safer.
But sometimes I wish I had been able
to toss it off, to show my starry shine
without being mortified for wanting to.
Still, even shrouded, I am silver.
This dazzle is my secret treasure,
an irrefutable brightness
in my own unseen eyes.

THE ONE WITH THE SOFTEST QUILT

Here, sweetheart.
Come, little ones— I know, honey.
Inside the cabinet, under the covers,
startled, frightened, anxious, dreading—
your fear comes in so many flavors
and I will hold them all.
Just being alive
is terrifying.
Hide your head in my lap.
Let me hold you tight, tight.
How many scared ones
will I tuck into bed tonight?
All of them, loves.
Every single one of us.

THE ONE WHO IS SUCH A WHITE LADY

Notes to myself.
Don't say:
This is not who we are.
Facts say: this is who we are and who
we've always been.
Remember in college when you suddenly realized
you were not the protagonist of your favorite books?
You were the other thing, the bad one.
Do not pretend the world is better
than you damn well know it is.
And yet our chest thumps stubbornly
that this is unacceptable.
Indeed.
So what are we going to do about it.

THE ONE WHO ALWAYS SAYS

THE WRONG THING

This is why I don't talk!
Look what happens,
I open my big mouth and
blah blah blah
disaster. Humiliation. Hurt feelings.
This is why I hide.
Better to stay in here.
Maybe I'm a miser but at least
I'm not making messes.
They sigh a little.
Hand me the mop.
Tell me to clean it up.
Afterward, they take my hand.
Bring me
back to the table.
Bring me bread,
give me soup,
slide over a spoon and tell me,
Why don't you say the blessing tonight.

THE ONE WHO REMEMBERS TO BREATHE

They all rush about,
cry, yell, swoon at their
own ideas, toddlers on the sand who
somersault, spill things,
try to clean them up but break them.
Storms roll through, big swells that
churn things up, tear them down,
roll away again.
I stay. Always here.
The inhale I'm not afraid to take,
the exhale I don't clutch to keep.
I am eternally generous with both,
unafraid to let them come and go.
Steady, again, in and out,
over and over.
I cradle the moon and the pearl.
I turn skeletons into sand.
I gleam with the ancient gleam
and I glimmer new each morning.
I crash through the banquet hall
I ebb out again.
Underneath everything,
eyes closed,
in and out,
over and over,
I am the ocean.

THE ONE NO ONE CAN HEAR

She is locked in her invisible soundproof
chamber yelling as loudly as she can.
Can anybody hear me??
No. We cannot see her either,
but we know she is there because of
the banging that jolts us sideways down deep
every now and then.
So we gather, blind, so she can see us.
Silent onlookers,
witness to her
invisibility.
At least we
keep her company.
At least she knows
we are here.

YOU CAN'T HEAR ME BUT I AM YELLING

dear one
I beg you
please don't require a tragedy
to wake you up to your life

THE ONE WHO IS A CAT

I accept all silk cushions,
adulation, livers, temples,
and treats.
I accept sunny corners,
laps, and the occasional
pleasure of a good rub.
Indulge me, coo at me,
pray to me, long for me—
go ahead.
Or put me in an alley.
I'll find delicacies
in every dumpster,
a friend in every tree,
and my claws are as sharp
as my teeth.
You are not a baby, kitten.
You're a goddamn cat.

THE ONE WHO STAYS

(AND HUMS THE SONG)

Oh but I could always go—
you understand that, right?
I could get on a plane train motorcycle,
sail off into the sunset, white scarf trailing—
or hell just take the car,
the one with all the carseats,
the cheerios on the floor.
Drive away and never come back.
I could.
I really could.
I'm free like that.
That possibility sits on my tongue,
the untasted sacrament.
But I choose this
particular glorious mess.
I stay because I want to.
Do you feel the humming power of that?
The ancient maternal planetary rotation?
Listen. No one can make me
do a damn thing—
but I will do anything for love.
Pour that on your cheerios.

THE ONE WHO THOUGHT

WE HAD A DEAL WITH THE UNIVERSE

Still.
I did everything right.
You told me to trust me and so I did.
I wrote the words,
I made the promise,
I kept it as hard as I could.
I did it.
I did the fuck out of it.
Because you told me that
if I just trusted,
it would all turn out all right.
And now it is not all right.
We are in trouble.
I thought you would keep your end
of the deal.
At least— I hoped.
I really, really hoped.

THE ONE WHO KEEPS IT ALL TOGETHER

Too hard.
Too long.
Too thankless, dishes, herding cats.
I don't know how much longer
I can

THE WORST ONE

This is so stupid.
You are so embarrassing.
Please erase that so no one sees it.
I can't believe you just wrote that.
Just bury it somewhere
so no one will see
I beg you
in the name of all that is holy.
Just don't expect so much.
You'll never be one of those.
There is no miracle waiting for you.
Let's just be clear that *that*
is never going to happen for you.
If it was going to,
it would have already happened by now.
You'd better grow up
and get yourself
a real job.
I know I'm being horrible,
but
take your hand off my shoulder
or I might cry and I can't do that.
I wanted everything, is all.
I wanted everything.

THE ONE BEHIND HER,

THE LITTLE BRIGHT SHINING ONE

I always knew there was no deal.
It won't all be all right.
Don't be afraid.
I am not afraid.

THE ONE WHO IS ABSOLUTELY FRANTIC

I took the risk, made the leap,
no net, no lap,
just rocks at the bottom.
I have an idea, an idea
I'm not supposed to say.
Maybe we should end it;
it's the only way, I cannot see another.
I have failed, failed,
failed beyond what we could ever
have imagined.
I can't take care of my family.
This is the only way left.
This way they will be
safe.
The life insurance money will protect them
since I cannot.

THE LOVE

Stay with me, honey.
Just stay with me.

THE ONE WHO HAS SEEN IT ALL

Don't be scared of her.
She is just afraid.
Come here, sweetheart.
Let me ask you something.
If it isn't going to be all right,
if there are no deals,
no guarantees,
what do you want to do anyway?
What do you want to do
if you know it might be an absolute
shambles?

THE ONE WHO IS CONTROVERSIAL

I have all your affairs in order.
I made the will;
I arranged the life insurance.
It was me who nudged you to write those letters
sitting in the back file, the ones to your family,
just in case.
You don't have to go,
but if you can't stay,
it will still be okay.
I know you need an escape hatch.
I know that I am the reason,
some days, you can
continue to
stay.

THE MANAGER MAKES

AN ANNOUNCEMENT

Settle down, folks.
She's fine.
Just a midlife crisis.
Confronting her own mediocrity.
Accepting that failure
might be the actual ending.
Most adults do.

ON BEHALF OF THE ONE WHO IS
STILL WEEPING LOUDLY

Don't stop her—
don't offer her sweets
or wine or tell a joke
or chin up.
Give her soft moss
on which to weep, give her
a stream to bathe in, give her
rain to keep her company.
Give her a bed, too,
warm by the fire, and
a stack of towels—
then leave her be
so she can cry herself to sleep
because later this evening
you will trip over the towels
in astonishment
for after she wails
she glows—
tears turned to pearls
her soul a luminous drop
her bed gone velvet
and how bright gold
the world
as she sleeps.

THE ONE WHO IS SCORNFUL

What a pathetic epiphany
to have at this age.
That life isn't fair?
That it doesn't work OUT for everyone?
Where have you been living, princess?
Did you think the universe
made a special DEAL with you?
Did you think it was going to hold you,
just you?
Oh my god, you did.
You did.

THE ONE WHO KEEPS THE FAITH

Nothing is as lonely
as being lost from myself.
It's dark
and we can't find each other.
But I hold a lamp,
even though only I can see it,
and it glows with
a soft certainty
that we will find ourself again,
that it will turn out
in spite of all appearances
we were all, always,
still here.

THE ONE WHO IS

OUR OWN PERSONAL MALEFICENT

I will bring the poison.
I will make the accusation.
Look what you did,
you softened,
you let down your guard, and
look what happened.
Disaster.
If you're going to stop pushing
and put us all at risk
with this magic and art and true love business,
it better be good.
And it is not good. Not yet.
I am afraid for them, do you understand?
No one else is paying attention.
Not even the one with the wagon.

MALEFICENT TELLS US HER SECRET

I keep watch. I always have.
You think of me as cold and cruel,
spikes always out.
But I have a job to do.
I keep watch.
Only the little one can tug on my cloak
and give me the nod.
Now? Are you sure?
So I pull back the curtain and there they are—
the flowers.
They've always been safe behind my sharpness,
pulsing, blooming, breathing and twining,
the most alive thing anyone has ever seen:
their own living vibrant
beautiful selves.
They do not speak.
They are already
blooming their eloquent hearts out,
and we do not need words
to know that they exist for beauty,
they are our own life force,
they are made of everything,
and everything hushes
in reverence.
I gaze up at them.
(When did I get so little?)
Aren't they beautiful?

We stand shoulder to shoulder,
all of us.
I announce,
If you fuck with the flowers,
I will fuck you up.
The one with the axe steps forward
and whispers,
If anyone fucks with the flowers,
I will fuck them up with you.

THE ONE WHO READS

THE MESSAGE ALOUD

The instructions from the flowers
are very simple.
(Shhh, stop asking me about money—
no they don't say anything about your taxes—
just finish the laundry later, for crying out loud—)
Ahem.
Okay.
Um— so— everything is holy.
Pay attention.
This must be the important part,
it's underlined:
Walk in awe the rest of your days.
No, that's all it says.
No really, that's all there is.
Well I don't know either.

THE ONE IN CHARGE OF RITUAL

I ask Maleficent,
What would you like to do
now that you don't have to guard the flowers from us?
She contemplates.
I would like to lie down next to them
because I love them
and maybe take a little nap.
So I make her a little nest of soft white linen.
And what would you like to use to
release your burdens—
fire, water, earth, or air?
She knows immediately:
Water.
And what sort of water would you...
But she has jumped already
into the stream.
I am wet from her splash.
Later, I tell her I love her the most.
She already knows.
We both smell like pollen.

THE ONE WHO GRABS THE ROPE

I'm not dignified, not graceful;
I'll lunge and blister my hands.
Everyone will say
I should do things more elegantly.
Twice I have left relationships
that were drownings.
Everyone said I should have
done things more elegantly.
When I was out,
when I could breathe again,
I was astonished how long I believed
it was just supposed to be like that.
How long I lived with
water in my lungs— but elegantly—
thinking that I was supposed to
like that.
It is not supposed to be like that.
I won't stand it here, either—
won't watch you gasp
and call it love.
Won't watch us die
and call it life.
Let me throw you a rope.
Stop gasping
elegantly.
You are made to pull yourself out.

THE ONE WHO UNDERSTANDS BIOLOGY

Tired honeybee,
if you race around like a hawk
the world will have
no honey.
Oh how we need your quiet hum,
your sweetness.
Beloved,
stop racing.
Adrenaline is
the wrong juice.
You were made to run
on nectar.

THE ONE WHO MOUNTS THE EXPEDITION

I finally realized who was missing.
It was the one who laughed for sheer joy,
at pansies. Yellow dress. Her!
She lived here once, so we go
to find her— hello?
you must still be here, I knew you once,
I will not give up on you.
What happened, dearheart? Where did you go?
Oh I am here, she whispers, eyes closed.
Right here, where you have been
sucking the life out of me.
She is drained and pale.
Right there— in the shadowy corner.
Set me free. Let me go.
Stop making me the life force for
all of you. It's too much.
We untangle her, stammer sorry
for the tubes, these bite marks.
Go get your own life force,
says the purple velvet pansy one,
pulling her purple velvet pansy cloak around herself,
face white.
She stalks out
into the night
and we cannot blame her.

THE ONE WITH THE TEETH

I'm horrified. Don't look at me like that.
I didn't mean it.
I didn't know that would happen.
I was just so hungry.
I was just trying to feed
everyone.

WE SIT IN THE AWKWARD SILENCE, AFTER

It is quiet in the room after the purple cloak
sweeps out.
Will it be just us now?
Just stone and wood?
No velvet, no color?
Will we ever laugh again?
One of us makes soup.
One of us brings in firewood.
One of us lights the candles.
We'll have comfort, then,
if we can't have joy. Solace,
if bleak.
But the quiet one has slipped outside
with pansy seeds
in her pocket.
We won't even know
until spring.

THE ONE WHO BLAZES

This galaxy in my chest—
to love a child
to cradle
to hold
to protect
to delight in
—oh most fierce
tenderness—
dawning at
first kick
first cry
first *Mama*
first time they barrel in for a hug
and it is my arms they fall into—
familiar sun
fiery star in my heart
stay close, now,
for it is dark
and when we are lost
I will follow your milky way.

THE ONE WHO IS BRAVEST

Watch me pick up the phone.
It's the dentist. Difficult.
Dial, then pull up the calendar
(headphones, such prowess)
take a deep breath.
Talk. Smile.
I sound just like a grownup.
Now I am laughing like a friendly normal person—
now I am typing things into the calendar—
oh my god oh my god
I did it.
Watch my hand shake as I
set down the phone.
Watch me raise my chin high
in exhausted triumph.

THE ONE WHO IS EVEN BRAVER

THAN THE ONE

WHO PICKS UP THE PHONE

Never fucking again
I vowed
but here I am again,
fuuuuuuuuuck.
To vow once again—
never again—
might be the bravest
kind of brave
we have.
Here I go—
to be unembarrassed
to try again
when I didn't want
to have to.

THE ONE WHO NUMBS OUT

ON INSTAGRAM

I watch as the soldiers—
but look at this adorable dress.
I watch as—
but maybe this green juice.
I watch as children go hungry,
and I do not get on a plane and take them my bread.
I don't even take it down the street.
I watch them shoot
person after person after person after person
but I don't put my own skin in front of the gun
even though I am a person too.
That is, I aspire to be a person. That is the goal.
I want to be a person I don't despise, one I can
live with, one I can look in the eye
and say
I saw it all, so here is bread, here is my body,
and here is my heartbreak, we grew kale and beans in it—
here is a village we raised from seed,
a law firm a bakery
a hospital a library
here is the theater
here is my row
and here are the roses
I brought to the show.

THE ONE WHO STILL CAN'T THAW

They bring her in still rigid from the cold,
fists melded to the edges of her sled,
all of her frozen from her
white-knuckled flight.
We thought she'd thaw quickly
in the warmth of our banquet hall,
we remembered her twirling and blooming,
but she only blinked and shuddered at the bright.
Lay her down outside, said the wise one.
Pour dirt on her. Trickle water—
gently, like that.
She needs to sleep in the garden
a whole season, at least.
She needs time undisturbed
down in the dark
with no one jostling her.
Only then can her fingers uncurl.
Only then can she put down roots.
Only with roots
will she ever bloom
into herself again.
To the frozen bulb of a woman she whispered,
Take your time. It's all right.
There are colors inside you still worth waiting for.
Some seasons need dirt not light.

THE ONE WHO HEARS THE SEA

In a concrete apartment block
floating in the dirty sky
she rushed silent in my heart,
a clamor of impossibility.
In the green city she called,
hours spinning webs with my girl
along highways home and back.
On the prairie I went under.
Closed my eyes and held my breath,
gritted my teeth to hear
the roar of her forever lost.
But then I gasped and opened my eyes.
Sat up, heard the waves
calling like clues in the infinite
sea of possibility—
not a mourning, but a pull,
an ode to hope, to going.
And now I hear her down the hill
every morning, walk my tea
down to the misty island
sea— and whisper, I love you
baby—
it took years of detours
but I finally made it home to you
(and me).

THE ONE WHO KEEPS TRYING

When I fell in love,
Madre said,
This is love, kid. Don't fuck it up.
But I did—
I fucked it up.
So I wail to Madre,
Ohhhhhh I fucked it up, and
I swoon dramatically to the floor,
like I am drunk from
poor boundaries
and codependence
and juice boxes.
But Madre laughs so hard
we both almost pee.
You did. You fucked it up so completely.
Madre cups my face.
I love you for it.
For fucking it up?
For trying anyway.

THE ONE WHO FUCKED IT UP

In my own defense, I fucked it all up
by trying too hard to be good.
Even though Mary Oliver said
I do not have to be good.
I tried to be good like the wild geese,
a good mother, good at laundry,
good in bed.
I used the word "resilience"
like a weapon against myself.
And I did not hold myself
precious.
I did not hold myself
hold tightly enough to my own
hold onto to my ownself.
But may I remind you that
I was trying to hold on to
six other whole people at the same time
and it was my first time
and they are hungry and wiggly
and they all need new shoes
and a hug.
So look.
I held on to my loves.
I did a thousand loads of laundry.

And yes, part of me slipped through
my stiff knuckles and the spilled juice
and my codependent boundaries
and by trying so hard
I fucked it all up and she got lost
in the snow. And I didn't tell anyone
because I knew you'd all be mad at me.
It was me. I did it.
Me my own self.
Can you have compassion on a beginner?
Can I?

THE ONE WHO BRINGS

A STUPID YOGA MAT

I am in a hotel room
with candles,
earl grey,
and a stack of paper.
I have gone away
to land back here at myself,
to pound feet
on my purple mat
but mostly to cry on it
until I can find my way
back to the solid ground
of my own self
to lick the sacred soil
of my lost parts
and grow a new familiar
in my own belly.

THE ONE WHO IS A FIRE DRAGON

This pool of solitude
has melted me—
I puddle, tears turning the lagoon
to salt.
The tight scaly crust of
holding it all together
cracks and shrieks
but finally dissolves in relief and steam.
The lagoon is a lake now—
now a sea—
I widen and widen
and then with a breath
the sun comes back on,
fiery star of my heart
the humming rises
and I am not afraid of its brightness going out
as I dive back in—
remember swimming,
remember laughter,
remember light flashing on the water—
I may be a fire dragon
but I have just remembered
that I am also
a water phoenix.

THE ONE WHO ALWAYS GETS US DRESSED

I step into the frothy dress,
shiny red mary janes.
There are not enough ruffles in the world
to cover up my sinfulness.
I pull on the linen shift from a catalogue:
a misplaced breastplate of righteousness.
There is not enough sackcloth anywhere
to cover up my teenage lusciousness.
I tie on a choker of old pearls.
A tank top so thin
my nipples announce themselves at last.
I buckle a brown belt of truth
around my tight jeans, cigarette in hand:
I wear my sin loudly
and she is glorious.
I am ripe for my own plucking.
I buy a fairy tutu, taupe,
(in Tokyo you can get away with such things
because fashion); I buy white wings,
I scrawl Vengeance Is Mine
across my skin and nude bodysuit.
Hardly anyone at the club
gets the joke.
I armor up, square shoulders, navy blazer
loose enough to hide my swollen belly.

I clasp on the mantle of adulting
before I burst out of everything.
I buy nursing bras made of steel
to hold in my milk, tight stretchy pants
that pinch me back into acceptability
among the men at the table.
I add scarves because my milk
leaks through anyway.
In the next world, me and my little girl
will pull on red rubber boots, like
a pair of tree spirits splashing in puddles and
watching the green park bloom.
Her fairy dress is pinker than mine was.
Briefly I clasped silk lacy things
around myself again
to heighten a desire already feverish
—turquoise emerald rose scarlet—
how bright and eternal
these butterfly wings.
I bought coats and gloves and horrible
numb boots and a thousand small snowsuits
and I cocooned under the downy puff
hoping
but not believing
winter would ever end.
Now I will buy clothes like art
even if they are out of fashion.

Here on this green island
I have dirt on the knees of all my jeans
and I trail goddess swaths behind me
however impractical.
I will pluck flowers with my bare hands
and hold them against my chest
or aloft—
the sword of my spirit
unsheathed and blooming at last,
a bodice of tenderness,
puffed peonies for sleeves.

THE ONE WHO MAKES HER

HILARIOUS PLANS

Nothing lasts as long as I think.
Twice now, in Tokyo and in Portland,
I have picked out apartments based on
school catchments
for a high school
my eldest now attends in a different country.
Just 15 more years of grueling early mornings
in this godforsaken land,
I thought in the prairie days, full of dread
and helpful thoughts.
My two year old spilled cereal; then the milk.
But my husband does mornings now,
and my eight year old is
an island kid, dragging a sea onion
everywhere he goes
like a seaweed tail.
What about taxes? Bills?
How the scary numbers get scarier and scarier
no matter how hard I
scrape my knuckles
on the bottom of the barrel of my courage?
Will it always be like that?

Obviously. Death and taxes,
in my (ever helpful) mind
they stretch ahead
forever and ever.
Taxes, anyway.
What about death?
How long does that last?
As long as my baby
was an infant?
Which is to say, the flutter
of an eyelash?
Or is it that we cannot remember death
because we stay there
so very briefly— a flash
before we dream again?

THE ONE WE TRUST THE MOST

I put my hand on my own chest.
I whisper into the banquet hall—
I've got you.
You're safe with me.

THE ONE WITH THE DRIPPY ROLLER

So, Madre, what do I do now?
She beams at me.
Go make life gorgeous, honey.
Isn't that what you say?
So go do that.
I think about the world, its problems,
its ugliness and horrors.
I feel willing, but daunted.
I picture my own kitchen:
peeling paint, cut-open wall,
pipes exposed.
Can I begin with my kitchen?
She looks at me so gently.
You may.
(Of course she corrected my grammar.)
She keeps going:
As long as you don't stop there.
That same day I buy daffodils
on the way home—
and a journal,
and paint.

THE ONE WHO MEANLY MAKES US
GO TO THE BEACH

It doesn't matter how much they puddle into
the goo of impossibility,
or how they can't find their gloves
or enough time, how they always try
to clean up the kitchen instead—
I am heartless.
We are going.
I pull on their sneakers.
Though they are not ready!
I grab a water bottle.
Though they are very busy today!
They're worse than the children, but I
open the door and we are out—
all the panicked ones taking deep breaths,
all the worried ones sending emails to themselves
so they don't forget things,
all the anxious ones feeling sheepish about
how out of shape we are.
All of us, hovering, and I shoo us along
out in the world, blinking, shivering,
protesting, bitterly cold and bitter! at being forced!
so cruelly! so meanly! so foolishly! away from all the
things! we have to do!
and then we are on the road, heading down,

and they keep up the resentment all the way
to the orchard but when they see the water
between the bushes
they crow and gasp and say
Oh!
Oh it is so beautiful!
Oh I am so glad we came!
Oh beach, I love you so!
Oh perhaps we should come tomorrow, too!
And I roll my eyes.

THE ONE WHO IS A SKEPTICAL WITCH

Things get blurry
and she wonders like Monet
if all magic is just
deteriorating eyesight—
say a false mirage
we draw over the unbearable grimness.
A story before sleep, before death.
A purple yoga mat to cry on.
A silk dress over the bandages.
A clean sheet flapping in the wind.
And would that be so terrible?
To take the veil or even the laundry
and let it flutter,
to shake loose the blooms we only see
when our daying
is tinged like rose petals
with our dying?
I could call that magic.
I could.
Go ahead, call it delusion,
or cataracts even—
go ahead, say transcendence is an illusion,
call it sentiment because
we are still here watching
all the little ones shimmer

along their pink petal edges that
they cannot even see
and oh—
the sun is setting gold now so
she will keep shaking the veil
and you can call that gleam
before it goes dark—
that glimmer, that spark—
well you can call it
honestly
whatever
the hell you want to
but she is calling the four directions
and stepping between time
and just between us,
between the trees and the sea and the circle,
we call it alchemy.
Which of course
is just another word
for you
and for me.

THE ONE WHO IS PAYING ATTENTION

This moment, here, this one exactly—
warm air like water,
bicycle beneath you,
this flying hum is how
sixteen feels—
and this, this head thrown back dirty laugh
in a dive bar, how sticky it is,
how the luscious smoke clings—
and this curve, this softness, this fuzzy head
against your cheek,
this tiny blinding sun on your chest,
don't miss it—
don't miss it—
the yellow braille dots as you wait for a train,
the water dripping off a hydrangea,
the dull gleam of a steel sink as you do dishes,
the piles of laundry,
that car you hated,
the sound when they laugh
and
the flapping wings go off inside your chest, oh—
that time I came to you
and whispered *This is love, don't fuck it up*
because you were so afraid
you almost missed it—

here it is, here, right now,
stop waiting to get to the good part,
be here for this messy moment,
don't miss it,
this one exactly—
the sun on your blanket,
this meandering story at book club,
the pile of shoes and bandaids again,
the quick hug,
all the bees like all the spirits
and all the blossoms
humming at you
just as hard as we possibly can.

THE ONE WHO HOLDS ALL THE OTHERS

My lap is a solar system.
Soft breasts, steady heart,
velvet arms with the
droopy elbow skin so comforting
to troubled fingers.
Oh honey, I say,
I know. Come here.
I've got you. Cry it out,
just like that— good, good good.
I'm right here.
Here I am, sweetheart.
I'm always right here.
Soft palm on cheek.
The slow thump on the back.
Everything you never got
is right here in your
own
soft
cosmic
lap.

THE ONE WHO ALREADY REMEMBERS

How quick it was,
how it flashed by—
a long endless sticky itchy tangle
of broken things,
trying to pull the beauty out
like hair from the drain
but as soon as it passed,
I cried, wait wait—
let me do it again, every
pile of bills, every scary
phone call, every diaper and load
of laundry, let me have
every awful thing
if only
to be human again—
oh let me be incandescent
in the humming world again

THE ONE WHO IS MORNING

—If this is life right now,
how will I rise to meet it?

Here I come, pattering down the path
to meet you, rising to the occasion
to the challenge
to a new day
like the sun
like the moon
like the mother levitating up
out of a dead sleep
because somewhere someone is crying.
Here I come, softer around the edges,
doughy and punched down,
yielding to the inevitable chemistry of yeasty
love, thrush, milky nights waiting up
for the babies who are now teenagers.
Here I come,
the star of the maiden in my eyes,
the bread of the mother in my belly,
the fire of wisdom in my hands.
After the dark night of the soul,
I always come.
I rise again and again to meet you, my life,
my beloved companion.

Here I come for the laughing crying bleeding digging
gushing wrangling stirring singing blooming
cradling mourning washing making
holding comforting telling
telling telling
all of it
something true rising up like the
soft loaf billowing under the tea towel,
the round hope that feeds us all.
Wait for me, loves,
here I come.

ACKNOWLEDGMENTS

You have to be quite foolish to write a book of poems when you are
not, technically, a poet.

For assisting me in this glorious foolishness, from the bottom of my
heart I thank the bright lights in my Patreon community, you
RichJuicyStarryBeautiful humans. I LOVE YOU SO MUCH. I
could never have written these poems if you all weren't there
to hold them, and me, with such sacred and utter tenderness. I
never knew that there were so many kindred spirits in the world,
and I am infinitely grateful to have found you all.

For being willing to share about such a vulnerable time in our lives, I
thank my husband, Nick North. For being my beloved, my lover,
and my best friend—and for seeing me—thanks for that too.
Thank you for being so generous and brave in countless unseen
ways in our life, and thank you for being in charge of rodents,
and thank you for loving me even as we grow and change and
our love and partnership do too. Forever and always and even
after that, my love.

For how I have certainly embarrassed you, I apologize in advance to
my children. Sorry not sorry.

For being the kindest and most capable midwife to this book, I
thank Kate Oliver. Not only did you design the gorgeous cover,
without your belief in these words I might never have been brave
enough to peel open my heart and turn it into print.

For showing me how to live my heart and my truth as fully and
lovingly as I am capable, and reminding me to laugh especially
when things are very serious, I thank my parents and siblings
and our whole weird wonderful family. Woof woof.

For cradling me and my beloveds with such bounteous kindness and
love, I thank the people and the plants and the spirits and the
animals and the land and the ancestors of Salt Spring Island. I
honor the sobering fact that we are on the unceded lands of the
Coast Salish people and I am so grateful to live and write and
dream in this beautiful place. Thank you.

ABOUT THE AUTHOR

Katherine North is the author of *Holy Heathen: A Spiritual Memoir*, the story of how she grew up evangelical but turned herself into a fairly foul-mouthed but extremely happy heathen mystic.

She's also the author of *The Secret Society of Saint Nicholas*, a story for kids (of all ages) who have received some very terrible news about Santa.

She created a process called The Queen Sweep, which helps sparkle-brains, creatives, and other interesting people navigate things like clutter, finances, paper, and to-do lists. This is a lot more fun than it sounds.

She and her husband, Nick North, made an award-winning documentary about their big queer blended family called Just Another Beautiful Family, and then they made a TV show about buying a house on a rural island sight unseen during the pandemic. They enjoy this sort of glorious foolishness too.

Find Katherine online:

http://KatherineNorth.com

Printed in the USA
CPSIA information can be obtained
at www.ICGtesting.com
LVHW051455190324
774867LV00004B/465